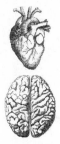

Before the First Kiss

Ashe Vernon & Trista Mateer

WORDS DANCE PUBLISHING
WordsDance.com

1st Edition
ISBN-13: 978-0-9979404-2-8
ISBN-10: 0-9979404-2-5

Cover design & interior layout by Amanda Oaks

Type set in Bergamo, Digory Doodles + Print Clearly

Words Dance Publishing
WordsDance.com

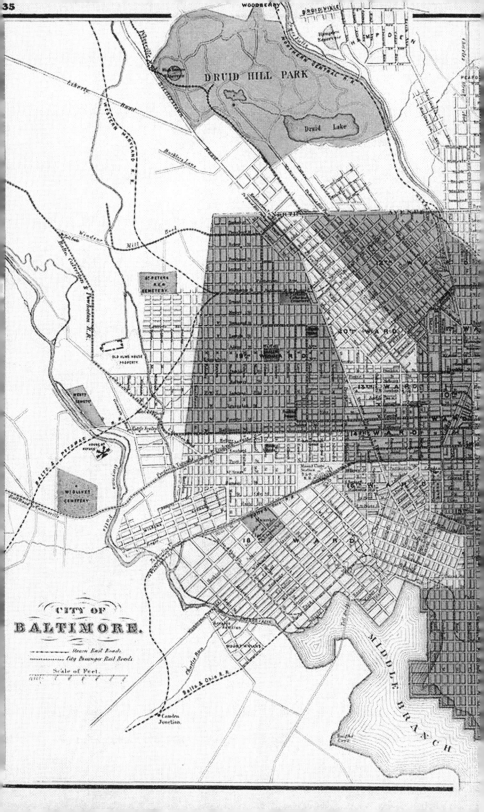

DRUID HILL PARK

Druid Lake

MIDDLE BRANCH

CITY OF
BALTIMORE.

Steam Rail Roads
City Passenger Rail Roads

Scale of Feet.

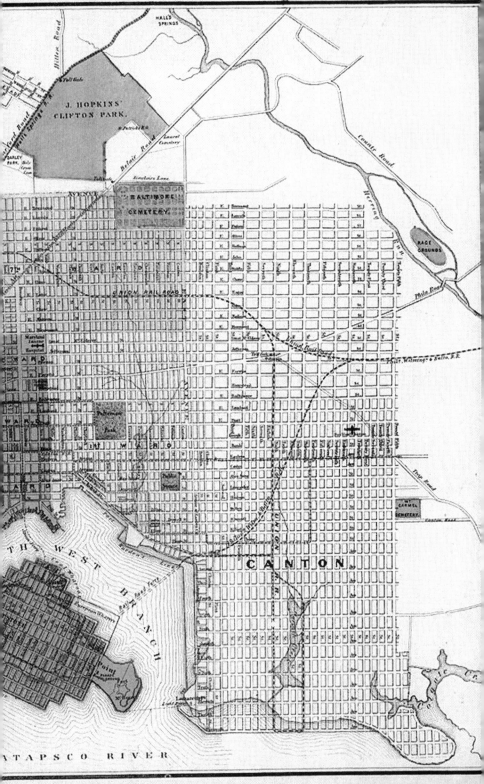

J. HOPKINS'
CLIFTON PARK.

BALTIMORE
CEMETERY

RACE
GROUNDS

MT CARMEL
CEMETERY

CANTON

H WEST BRANCH

PATAPSCO RIVER

For her.

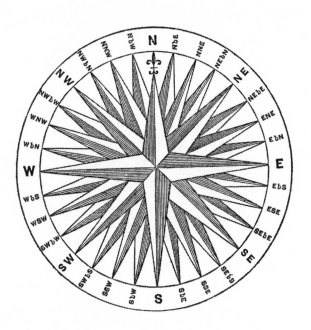

INTRODUCTION
by Ashe Vernon

Everyone's got something to say about dating a writer. All of it is vague and unhelpful, and most of it bounces between "AVOID AT ALL COSTS" and "achieve obscure immortality through the shit they have to say about you." What I don't ever hear anyone talking about is what happens when you're both writers: that bizarre, intimate feedback loop of feeling and language that you can create together.

This book is our feedback loop. It's nonfiction: our story as best as we could tell it. The process of collaborating on a work of art about something this close-to-home has been strange and enlightening and stressful and painful and important.

This is the most honest piece of work I have ever been a part of. It's everything we have. Everything we were and everything we wanted and everything that's left. We hope that it means something to you.

Despite everything, we're trying.

Before the First Kiss

Ashe Vernon & Trista Mateer

Before the First Kiss

Trista Mateer:

GOOD DOG
after Marty McConnell

I do not want to fall in love with you.
I'm trying to train my heart like a good dog.
All spraying myself in the face with water. All treats
when I don't want to do cartwheels at the sound of
your name. All well-meaning violence. All *bad girl!!*
All *I said NO!* All heavy handed. All *HEEL.* All *STAY.*
All *DON'T BITE THE HAND THAT FEEDS YOU,*
just bite everything else.

Ashe Vernon:

HALL OF MIRRORS

You say,
girls fuck me up,
and I become furious child,
tearing up fistfuls of grass:
this wet, heaving thing
that wants to scream,
I AM NOT HER, I AM NOT HER, I AM NOT HER,
until you actually believe me.

I get it.
She was soft, too.
She stung, too.
She was wide hips and lush mouth and
I'm peeking over your shoulder
like her ghost.
I get it.

But I can't compete with your
second-hand heartbreak.
I won't start fights I already know
I'm going to lose.

Trista Mateer:

WANTING HER

The poets say "love" like it's synonymous with "tender"—
I don't know how to want like that anymore. Everything is
tooth and nail, everything is visceral. All instinct and no logic.
I compare all my lovers to fruit so I can rip them apart.
What does that say about how this will end? Still, wanting her—
feels like a stomach ache & a fever, feels like doing the one thing
I know I'm not supposed to do, feels like another brick through my
window but at least I know this one is coming. There might be
fear stuck in my throat but at least it's coated in honey.

Ashe Vernon:

BABY

She likes when you call her *baby*
and you like the way she likes it.

How you want her isn't so much electric
as it is a slow burn at the tips of your fingers.
You've lost sleep thinking about her mouth.

She's this buzz in your blood like
the radio down low and
humid nights in midsummer;
all young love and
messy ponytails and
sweat at the nape of the neck.

You want to kiss her and
you've convinced yourself
that's all there is to it.

Trista Mateer:

SWEET TEA AND SEVEN OTHER TEXAN CLICHÉS

So my girl

might taste like
fear of change;

might taste like spurs without the boots, without the cowboy;
might taste like sweet tea and seven other Texan clichés.
I'd have to buy a one-way nonstop to find out.

All I know for sure is that
she writes a lot about religion
for someone who looks out of place in a pew.
She subscribes to the bible of mouth to mouth
(and gin, and sweat).
She makes me want to ransack my own temple.

My girl says, *come on, baby, lay it on me*
and I still don't know if she's talking about my story

or my mouth.

Ashe Vernon:

LONG DISTANCE FLIRTATION 101

She says, *I want to kiss you.*
I say, *okay, but just so you know,*
it's a shit-show, over here.
It's always better in theory,
isn't it?

She says, *no strings attached,*
like she doesn't know that I am all puppet,
that I am gawky marionette, that
I wear "casual" like someone else's jacket.

(But I'll take what I can get.
After all, I don't know what
to do with her heart, yet.)

Trista Mateer:

AWKWARD POET TEXTS LONELY POET AT 1:01AM ON A THURSDAY

I retype these texts at least three times
before I send them because I want them
to sound like the poems I keep trying
not to write about you. (1/6)

Not that you don't deserve poems or
anything. You deserve poetry; believe me.
But it seems like such a weird thing to
give to a poet. (2/6)

Would you still bring a florist flowers on
a date? I don't know. And anyway, what
if you don't like my metaphors? Look,
I know you (3/6)

don't need anything fancy from me. I know
when it comes down to it, peel back the
soft fleshy exterior and all we're left with
is heart. (4/6)

I know that's why we keep writing over
and over. An attempt at baring our chests
to somebody else. What I'm trying to say
is that (5/6)

tenderness isn't something you know how to
ask for. I get it. I still want to give it to you.
I just don't want it to come out wrong. (6/6)

Ashe Vernon:

BUZZ AND HUM AND YOU AND YOU AND YOU

I wasn't supposed to chase you,
but here I am: imagining my hands in your hair.
I'm caught in the sideways tumble of your laugh,
your small hands and how they cradle my heart
like a butterfly net. I thought I could
outrun this,

but I'm going soft at the edges.
Where there should be bone, there is
honey. There is drip. There is sweet.
Where there should be spine, there is
hive. There is hum. There is buzzing.

It's swarming season, and the bees will
pour like water through your fingers. They
have forgotten their stingers.

I've forgotten my sting. I'll drink sugar water
from the palm of your hand, if you let me.

Trista Mateer.

GIRL OR QUIET TREMBLE?

I show up with hydrangeas and kiss you
with more teeth than lip and you taste like
toothpaste and grin. You pour sugar straight
into my open mouth and then it's just skin
and touch and heart pulsing away like I want
to run but I never do. That's how I know it's
a dream. My heart is so full of maybe, I can't
even get away from it when I sleep.

Ashe Vernon:

I NEVER MENTIONED

I spend weeks peeking over my shoulder,
refusing to look fear in the eye.
Instead, I text you for days on end
and build myself into exactly the person
I want you to look at. It's different than poetry.
It's less honest.
I ignore the voice that wants to know if
your kisses would taste like that boy in London—
the one you never told me the name of.
The one who is
six years of your life while I
am just passing fantasy.
Still, a thousand miles away, you are
safe.
I pretend not to think about reality
crashing in around us, or
what would happen if, in person, we become
unoiled clockwork gears: if we click and click and grate—

if the first kiss isn't worth it.

Trista Mateer:

AFTER HOURS

At the end of a seven-hour shift,
I am mostly tuning out the discussion
my coworkers have around me.
I know all the usual horror stories:
bad tips, lousy customers, food dropped.
Still, I almost always
lean into the conversation to say,
hey—
remember that time a woman
threw her lobster at me? Or
that time I spilled a tray of drinks
on a mother on Mother's Day?
But tonight, I don't.
Tonight, I am too busy texting this girl.

When someone asks who I'm talking to,
I say, *no one.* I say, *it's nothing.*
I say, *well it's not nothing but it's not something.*

They say, *you've got a heart*
next to her name in your phone.
It sure looks like something to me.
I shake my head,
but

I blush the whole drive home.

Ashe Vernon:

A RESPONSE POEM

I have no idea what to call this
thing that you do to me—this
upside-down tremor of an almost-earthquake
at the pit of my stomach.
Science made a mistake when it didn't
mark your mouth as a point
on the Richter Scale.
And now, I am all tremble and chaos
holding my breath for you:
us, just two girls with summer wrapped
around our throats. No—
you as the epicenter,
you as ground zero,
you as all the ways I didn't know
I could be tied into knots—no,
tied into bows. You
as poet and tequila and
the early hours of the morning where
we are least afraid to talk to each other.
Me: self-conscious and wanton, deleting
all the dirty pictures I want to send to you,
deleting all the soft confessions I want to
share with you, coveting the parts of my chest
I don't know if I'm ready to give to you, yet.
What I'm saying is, it kills me
that we keep on writing about each other, but still
have no idea how to talk about it.

Trista Mateer:

THE ONE I DON'T SHOW YOU UNTIL AFTERWARDS

The first girl I loved ruined me for everyone else.

At least, that's what I tell everybody. That's what I tell myself when I don't feel like dealing with the truth of things, which is that I am the one who ruined me.

I threw myself too hard into it. Put myself through the wringer for a girl who didn't even like the taste of my name. Of course it ended on asphalt. I chipped my teeth on every poem she wrote about me, promised myself I'd do better, promised myself I'd stay safe even if that meant running.

Now it means never picking up the phone and placing the call that rings in your bedroom where I am steadfast on the line and ready.

AN EXERCISE IN PERMANENCE

Over drinks, I tell my friend
I just want to go out and kiss girls, but
what I really mean is I want to
book a flight to Baltimore and kiss you.
This isn't anything new.
I've been trying to close the distance
between our teeth for the last
six months—keep dropping *baby*
like a hint, like a trail of breadcrumbs, like a prayer.
I've always been pointed toward you,
even when it looked like I wasn't.
For a while there, in the middle,
there was the boy who quoted Neruda and made
pretty promises he had no intention of keeping.
There was the woman from Houston, with her
long legs, her sideways smiles, her body and the music
and the dark.
There were half a dozen botched dates:
the girl who picked me because my best friend was taken,
the boy who kissed and cried and never stopped talking,
the one who looked nothing like his profile picture,
the boy with the girlfriend, the girl with the boyfriend.
But there was always you.
My summer girl.
My blooming heat.
There was always you.

Trista Mateer:

POINTS A AND B

So there are two plane tickets in front of you.

One is new. It will carry you south into the hands
of a Texas desert. Red dirt, red sky, all blood & blush.
Summer even when it's not. A mouth on the other end
will say things you're not sure you can say back yet,
but it will say those things so damn good. All spine shiver,
all warmth, all promise and promise and promise.
Your mother will be so mad she'll stop setting a
place for you at holidays but it almost won't matter
because there's so much breath on your throat.

One is older. It will steer you straight into the center
of a postcard city. Rain and fog and cobblestone.
Trench-coat weather and off-peak trains. A red plaid scarf,
two coffee cups or maybe just one. The mouth on this end
is less reliable but you already went and made yourself
comfortable inside of it. It says *I adore you, I fucking
adore you* and you melt like a sugar cube into afternoon tea.
You've been dreaming of pulling this off for years

but now your heart feels like a fisherman's net.
It wants to keep everything that gets caught inside of it.

LONDON

Ashe Vernon:

POINT B

There are two plane tickets in front of you.

I am wound into a spindle of hope and near-misses.
We spend weeks joking about how
you could never take the Texas heat.
Still,
something ties fisherman's knots
in the lining of my stomach
when you go and put a whole ocean
between us.
There is no red dirt in London.

I would have met you on the bridge.
But I'm sorry
that he didn't.

Trista Mateer:

(I'M STILL HURTING)

I am stacking up the cups of my grief and knocking them down.
I made a drinking game out of it with some strangers in London.
Played it with gin in Glasgow. Sorrow looks so good on me.
I know every way to dress it up, even when I'm just working out
of a suitcase.

At home it is a little harder to keep the lonely at bay.
I spend a full month sleeping at the foot of my own bed.

Everyone says they're sorry it didn't work out.
I say, *I'm sorry too.*

I knew the mess going into it.
I adored the mess
but I was done with being haunted by a possibility.
Two people headed straight for each other at full speed
until one swerved out of the way and stopped answering the phone.
I played a game of chicken with a man who couldn't love me
and I won.

Everyone says they're sorry it didn't work out.
I say, *it's okay.* I say, *you can get a bottle of tequila delivered to your doorstep
at midnight in London.* I say, *I picked a great city to break my own heart in.*
And everyone laughs and I laugh and nobody is in on the joke.

Ashe Vernon:

AFTER LONDON

After London,
we agree that you shouldn't
come straight to see me, even though
it is the hardest surrender I've ever waved
a white flag for. Practically,
I know better than to be the arms you
bounce back in, but
I want to kiss his name out of your mouth.
I want to put my hands all the places he didn't:
suck on your fingers until you melt into something
so sweet, he looks like
lemon wedge and salt quarry, by comparison.
I want to dip you in milk and honey, take
hot tea body shots off your sore muscles,
your aching heart. I don't say any of this.
I watch you write his poetry; I know
that it's necessary, but I think of you:
three margaritas in, drunk texting me
at two in the morning and I want nothing more
than to lick the salt
from your lips.

Trista Mateer:

FIGHTS LIKE THIS ONE ONLY MAKE SENSE TO THE PEOPLE INSIDE OF THEM, or POEM IN WHICH I TELL YOU THAT YOU RUINED EVERYTHING YET STILL PROCEED TO DAYDREAM ABOUT YOUR HANDS IN MY HAIR

The first time we spoke on the phone, it was such a new thing. You & Me. The completely incredible idea of it. Two girls with summer stuck in our throats, everything was coming out warm. You read me your favorite Richard Siken poems. I kept thinking about your mouth in the dark. If it would wrap around me the same way it wrapped around words: with the deftness of a theatre major and the lightest touch of tongue.

The last time we spoke on the phone, it was all distance. It was a gas station roadmap from Baltimore to Austin ripped to shreds in the passenger seat. It was more than state lines spread out between us. It was dirt kicked up, bed sheets on the ground, trust thrown out with last month's poetry. You were on a break at work and you called to apologize over and over, because I am the kind of person who makes people feel the need to apologize over and over.

Unforgiving, maybe.

Hard when I wanted to be soft.

I don't know.

Things just never go the way I think they will anymore. Who would have thought I'd be the scissors? I always wanted to be the lace.

Ashe Vernon:

WHEN THE BEE STINGS BY ACCIDENT

So they're useless apologies.
So they're nothing but
buzzing in my mouth. So
I sit in the backroom at work
between an industrial sink and
a tower of boxes and talk and
talk and talk and talk and you
have nothing to say to me.

I told you I'd never hurt you
the way the last girl did.
I kept that promise.
I found a new way
to hurt you.

In the end,
I still proved you right.

Trista Mateer:

HONEYBEE REDUX

When I fall asleep
thinking about kissing you,
I am dragging the past around
by its ankles.

I swear I've told someone
this story before.

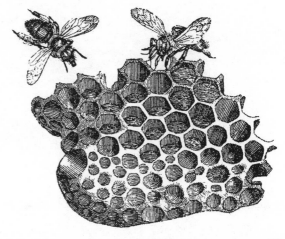

THE BOY IN MY BED

By the time I half-accidentally mention him to you,
I already know exactly how he tastes, how he touches,
which is more than I can say about you. Later,
I will resent all the words you hid underneath your tongue.
This will be different from resenting you.
By now, I am so starving for some kind of physical affection.
For confirmation of intent. After our very first date,
he calls me *lovely*. He smiles and covers his eyes
and whispers, *if you could just—stop looking at me like that,*
so I can find my sea-legs, again.
It feels like poetry.

I've spent so many months hungry for you. Maybe
I'm trying to prove some kind of point—that I don't
need you or that I don't have to stay tangled in our
twisted up love story: that I am capable of moving on
from you. I send you pictures of him and pretend not to be
self-conscious while you pretend to be excited.
I don't understand the rules of this thing we made
between us. You say, *You and your tiny bird boys,*
and it feels like an apology.

At this point in the story, our feelings are still
unspoken, like a corked bottle of champagne we
won't stop shaking. The word love starts to fizz
at the back of my throat and I've already
promised myself to swallow it.
I can only carry so much waiting.
You are six months of
it's casual until I say it isn't.
And you never say it isn't.
But we both know, I think.
At this point in the story, he is still lit
in the glow of a good first date.
He's not quite a person, yet: still out-of-focus,

like a walking daydream. He is soft hands,
soft touch, soft mouth—except
I can't write about anyone's mouth without
thinking about yours. Maybe that's why,
at this point in the story, I haven't
written my first poem for him. But the ones
I write for you are still just unanswered shots in the dark.
A month or two from this,
I will hold your heartbreak in both hands and
I won't know what to do with it. You'll be spilling over
like a broken faucet, saying all the things I spent
so many months waiting to hear. I
will be struggling not to shake into some kind of
avalanche when I say,
If you'd only told me,
this would have changed
everything.

Trista Mateer:

A BREATH, HELD

For weeks, I have fallen asleep thinking about
the space she would take up under my sheets, her body
like a second sun in my bed with all that warmth.
I want to bury my face in her neck
but my heart is so tired.

When she texts me about the new boy,
I do nothing with the words I've kept close to my chest
over the past couple of months. At this point,
there is no way to make it not sound like jealousy.
I don't want anyone to draw comparisons between this aching
and the way a child feels
when someone else picks up their discarded toy.
I never want her to feel second choice or backup plan.
She deserves someone close and quick to the draw.
And I want to let her have it.

I ask if they've kissed yet and she says, *oh
we've done a lot more than that.* I have no right to get choked up,
but I stumble anyway. The bed seems so much colder
when I'm not thinking about her hands.

Ashe Vernon:

THE ONE I DON'T WANT YOU TO READ

I am trying to put a pin in this.
I am trying to call this finished, or
over, or
something we are on the other side of.
But it's hard finding closure when we're standing
in front of a door we never opened.
See, you can't finish a race if you're still
standing, bashful, at the starting line.
Look at all the months we've already spent
watching each other fall in and out of love
with other people.
I wonder
if I'm meant to spend a lifetime
asking god about your mouth.
This boy is not my answer
to the question we never ask each other.
No matter what anyone says,
I'm not looking for you, in him.
He is not the echo of your hands;
he looks nothing like your ghost.
I shouldn't have to apologize
for the state we find ourselves in, and yet
I catch myself dusting my own heart
for fingerprints, for motive,
for evidence of a crime.
So this is what it is to be in love at a distance:
measured in miles,
measured in time-zones,
measured in how often I've thought
about my hands and your hands and
your hips and my thighs,
measured in how high we can stack
the fear, the denial, the regret.
I guess this is us finding out the hard way
that a hundred thousand maybes
aren't worth a single fucking
yes.

Trista Mateer:

A HUNDRED THOUSAND MAYBES

So put a pin in this.
Call it finished, or
over, or
something we are on the other side of.
Say the door was never swung wide,
but don't say it wasn't ajar.
Don't say I didn't spend nights
checking airline prices.
Maybe it doesn't count
if those nights were also spent
in other people's beds.
I'm not sorry for the months we passed by
loving other people.
Maybe I should be,
but every other bed led to this one.
I guess that would have made a stronger point
if I wasn't writing this at home alone,
a thousand miles away from
you, but
what I'm trying to say is:
you never had to ask god about my mouth.
You just had to ask me.

Ashe Vernon:

[REDACTED]

I don't care whose bed you were in.

So the door was ajar, and I
didn't walk through it, either.
But I was right there, baby,
I was right there.
I was on the other side, pushing
poems through the gap,
treating your name like a sonnet
or a symphony.
Don't tell me I wasn't
soft and open and ready.
Don't tell me I didn't spend all that time
waiting.

Don't tell me you didn't know
what I was doing.

I said I had my arms open for you.
You never told me you were
running to them.

Trista Mateer:

CRUSH

I spent the end of the year gathering up heartbreak like skipping
stones / marbles / pearls for a string / I just wanted to bite down on
something that wouldn't give / press my tongue to the cold / and
look at her / look at her / finally giving me something to break my
teeth on.

Ashe Vernon:

COLD SEASON

I didn't want to be
your newest breakup poem:
long-distance heartbreak,
four am text message apology.
Us summer-struck girls
aren't doing so well
in the cold.

Trista Mateer:

AN ADMISSION, LATE AND VIA TEXT MESSAGE

I tried carving out the parts of myself
that I wanted you to touch.

It's just,
there's so much more than I expected.

Ashe Vernon:

WITHOUT YOUR SIDE OF THE STORY

I couldn't wait for you, anymore.
I thought I was doing the right thing,
I swear to god. I thought
I was being brave when I untied the knots
in my heart and promised not to stand
in the wings of my own love story.
I spent weeks convincing myself that this
was the only option, that you
were still nursing a heartbreak in London,
that I
was never going to have your full
and undivided attention. I really thought
this was the only outcome.
I didn't know.
I didn't know.

Trista Mateer:

THE POET HIGHLIGHTS A CHARACTER FLAW

gasping in the dark at the thought of your soft / hell-bent on riding
this into the ground / I know it is too late to lose my breath over the
way your heart grins before it eats / and I do it anyway / reaching for
fruit only after it spoils / safety in the hesitation / it is easy to want to
call now that I'm not sure you want to answer.

Ashe Vernon:

ON FALLING IN LOVE WITH SOMEONE NEW WHILE YOU ARE STILL IN LOVE WITH SOMEONE ELSE

If he is like hot towel
to sore muscles,
then she
is sugar-chaser to straight shot
of tequila. They both

keep me warm at night.

I worry
that I have no right
to so much
heat.

Trista Mateer:

BECAUSE I OWE YOU ONE

YOU as a long drive through the desert, sunset in the Midwest.
YOU as a cold glass of water to parched lips.
YOU as the flowers and the hive.
YOU as every soft, late night I was full of hesitations.
YOU as velvet, fresh coffee, pen ink, breath hot against my throat.
YOU as sweet tea and the seven other Texan clichés
I couldn't come up with
when I wrote my first poem about you.
YOU as the fists and the fistfight,
the winner with bruised knuckles,
and the loser slunk off to suck on their wounds.
YOU as bruises, you as bandage, you as my sore ribs.
YOU as anxiety attack and quiet promise.
YOU as poet, preacher's daughter, small barista,
fine-arts-degree-holder, worst excuse for an inside voice.
YOU as dream girl.
YOU as emotional disaster zone.
YOU as radio tower down, communication issues, storm warning.
YOU as dream girl again.
Girl stuck on the sidelines.
Girl left waiting in the wings.
No.
Girl at the center of it all.
Even when you're writing about our goodbye,
my stomach still does flips.

Ashe Vernon:

QUESTIONS

If I keep writing poems about you
and no one ever knows that you read them,
are they still self-indulgent?
I mean, a tree falling in a forest, right?
How do I tell the nonbelievers that love
only ever made sense in poetry, or
that our unraveling was one
of the most romantic things
that's ever happened to me?
When am I supposed to stop talking about it?
How many ripples in the lake do I create
if I skip stone after stone after stone and
every one of them sounds like your name?

Trista Mateer:

ANSWER

I don't know about the lake,
but every time you say my name
you make ripples
in me.

Ashe Vernon:

SKINNY BOYS WITH BEAUTIFUL HANDS

In walks this boy:
all hipbone and jawline,
all crinkle-eyed smile.
For the first time in years,
I'm remembering what it is
to have the rug yanked
out from under me.

But then there's me:
all this skin I was born into,
all this body, always spilling over.
I am trying to be the woman
who wears her body in double digits
but does not dress her mouth in apologies.
But there's this boy, and it turns out
that those angel-boned wrists
are all it takes to bring my temple
to the ground.

By now, I'm carrying two decades of self doubt
in my back pockets: a lifetime of being warned
against becoming too much woman,
too much body.
And in walks this boy:
skinny hips and pianists hands. Suddenly,
every kiss raises questions I'm afraid
to put words to. Those hands
find my stomach and I have the good sense
to feel ashamed.

(I have preached self love to anyone
who would listen, only to be proven
hypocrite, snake in the grass,
unbeliever in the pulpit.)

But he is still here.
Fear sits under my skin,
hot and gangrenous, but
there is no part of me he is afraid to touch.
I don't feel big in his bed.
He leaves me honey gold and light.
Nobody says my name
the way he does.

After a lifetime feeling flavor-of-the-week,
maybe this,
maybe he,
marks the beginning of believing
in my own permanence.
Maybe this is where I declare myself
inherently valuable
and dare him
to prove me right.

Trista Mateer:

HYMN FOR AN OPEN MOUTH

Ask me about the summer
I fell in love with someone
more blackberry bramble than girl.
Aching to be touched
but never talking about the thorns.
And me, all heavy handed
and too proud to acknowledge
the things I'd cut myself on.
I dreamt about juice
running down my chin
for months.

Ashe Vernon:

TIME-ZONES

i.
It's two AM where you are.

ii.
We're writing our own hearts into bad punchlines, laughing about our broken love poems: the way we keep drawing maps to each other and giving them to strangers. We're so desperate for someone to know. We drag the same four metaphors in the mud behind us until they look dirty enough to feel like home.

iii.
Ten minutes later and we splinter into sobbing, crying over each other's hands: the way we cheated each other out of all this good before we even started. How we never got our honeymoon (but still there was all that *honey*, wasn't there?) just skipped straight to the divorce.

iv.
Funny, how you can knock a love story out of sync. How it shatters with the gentlest of taps.

v.
I'm trying to come to terms with the fact that I will probably never stop wondering how you kiss. I'm trying to come to terms with the fact that I will probably never find out.

Trista Mateer:

PAPER TRAIL

I want to write the poem that says *don't come to terms with this.*
The poem that sobs and doesn't know anything about letting go.
The poem that says *baby, please. I'm sorry that I'm so late.*
I'll get on the plane, I'll get on the plane, I'll get on the plane.

I want to write the poem that says *moving on was a good choice.*
The poem that sighs before it cuts our strings politely.
The poem that says *I don't mind that it didn't work.*
You're the kindest place I ever wanted to run towards, even if I didn't.

I need this one to be both.

So my voice cracks on your name and I cry thinking about your cheeks.
This is what's left:

My stubborn girl. All spit and buzz. So much fight in one tiny person.
You carry around more than anyone should ever have to.
I wanted to be the place you put everything down,

but it's okay if I'm not.

Ashe Vernon:

A POOR EXCUSE FOR AN APOLOGY

Listen—
Love and I have an ugly history.
Love is a tinderbox of empty promises.
It's five years of five hour phone calls.
All the times I took "good enough" because I didn't think "great"
would ever have me. Love is all the times I settled.
It's how I went trailing after mouths that didn't want me.
Love is colored by how often I've been willing to fall to my knees
and call impermanence some kind of holy.
Love is how everything is perfect until it isn't.
Love has always been distance and distance and distance. At least you
were actually miles away from me and not making a new country
on the other side of the comforter. At least we had a reason.

Trista Mateer:

IMPRESSION, SUNSET

Dream girl is happy in the arms of a skinny boy with beautiful hands and I am reading poetry about her new boyfriend as a reality check.

It has me listing off the things that will never happen because of distance and bad timing: her palm soft on the side of my face, glasses clicking together when we try to kiss, having to explain to my mother that I went and fell for a poet from Texas with a heart like a rose at the center of a sticker bush.

I hold hands with every could-have-been before I let it go.

All those blue days painted golden and smeared with orange.
All those lip prints blurred like a Monet on pillowcases and shirt collars.
Dream girl with all her sunset and that jawline.

THE CITY OF ATLANTA

Ashe Vernon:

NO MORE CRYING IN AIRPORTS

Sometimes, this thing we had seemed more
daydream and hearsay. Like the distance turned us
actors in a story and not real people
tying knots in each other.
It was so
poetic
to love in two different cities.
It was so
safe.

When your mother kicked you out,
I came up with a hundred different ways
to ask you to move in. With me. In Texas.
Way one hundred and one was me
offering a couch to sleep on,
only that wasn't what I meant. Or—
it is what I meant, but I left out the rest.
It seemed like so much to ask.
I didn't want to be
just another person
demanding more
than you knew how to give.
A couch
was safe.
We were good at safe.

I should have asked you to get on the plane.
I hope you can forgive me
that I didn't.

Trista Mateer:

THREE SEPARATE TRUTHS

1.
When my mother wanted me out
and you invited me to stay on your couch,
I couldn't figure out a way to say
the couch was just so far
away from you.

2.
The first time you called me *baby*,
I moaned so loud I woke my dogs.

3.
I hope you know
you don't have to ask my forgiveness
for anything.

Ashe Vernon:

AFTERTHOUGHTS

I still remember how you called me your girl in poetry.
This was a few months before you
boarded a plane that wasn't pointing towards me and
I didn't ask you to change direction.
You had something you had to finish,
a boy whose love hadn't broken you yet.
But you called me *your girl*
and I went all pop rocks and pink fireworks.
I'd have bloomed in the palm of your hand
if you'd asked me to.

Trista Mateer:

NOW EVERYONE IS IN ON THE JOKE

I want to pin up every word you write about me
so I can sit back and take it all in, spend nights
perusing over everything we delicately fucked up.

How we were on track, until we weren't.
The glass shattered before I even knocked it off the counter.

It's funny, isn't it?

We can look back on this and laugh about the time
we almost fell in love with each other, or did
but didn't want to say it.

We can laugh and laugh and laugh and laugh
and you'll keep writing about pop rocks and fireworks
and I'll keep feeling like I have legs made of blackberry preserves
when I read your poems or hear your name or
think about airports.

Ashe Vernon:

LONELY POET GIVES UP ON PRETENSE

I'll call it love for the both of us.

Trista Mateer:

THE POET HOLDS TIGHT TO PRETENSE

Go ahead. Call it love. Call it sunshine and soft, pink underbelly turned up. Call it romantic. Sugar-spun. Warm and tingling. Moth-to-the-light. A little bit of teeth. I always liked your poetry. The way you could make something that hurt seem so pretty.

Ashe Vernon:

NOTHING ABOUT THIS IS PRETTY

When you and the girl you accidentally fell in love with come to terms with everything you actually lost, it will be too late to fix things. You will dress it in poetry and call it progress. It will be no one's fault. There will be a boy in your bed who likes you enough not to leave, but who doesn't seem to be trying very hard to stay. You won't tell her about how, some days, he feels like a slow motion avalanche, because the rest of the time he feels like a dog-eared hymnal and you've spent enough of your life treating love like gospel. You won't drag your doubts to her altar. You won't rub salt in an already open wound, won't let her feel second best or backup plan or afterthought. So you spend weeks softly aching over two hearts instead of one. You eat your own when it starts beating too hard.

You just want a moment of quiet.

Trista Mateer:

DRAMAMINE

When you and the girl you accidentally fell in love with spend an hour talking about her new love and all the ways it does and doesn't function, you joke about wanting to lie on the kitchen floor. Flushed cheeks to cold tile. You crawl out of bed while she types and spill onto the bedroom floor instead because it's closer and you need to lay your face down somewhere you've never written a poem about her. She says she's worried about hurting you like she doesn't know this whole book is one big paper cut. It reminds you of the ocean, all this back and forth. It reminds you of that time you swam out too far in the Potomac River and almost couldn't get back in. So she's talking about her feelings and you're fighting for the shore. So she's saying _this is so fucked up_ and you're calling her _buddy_ in an attempt to keep it casual, and now you feel like you're going to throw up like a sick dog on the carpet by your bed.

Ashe Vernon:

THE BRIDGE, PART 2

For the last six months, she has been the one
you tell everything to. She has been
the open palms, the heavy-handed messiah.

Now, you are standing at the bridge with
your bedsheets in your arms. You're
holding yourself together with nothing but
maybes and chewing gum.

She is the current, or
she is the bridge, or
she is the place where
the tide comes in.

She tells you, *you said it's too late, but it isn't,*
and you feel like a tower of sand
collapsing in on itself.

Where you thought there was love, there is desert.
Where you thought there was desert there's
this ocean of love

and you're in too deep not to drown in it.

Trista Mateer:

DROPPING THE TORCH

She doesn't want you to wait for her.
She says it kindly but it doesn't feel kind.
There's vodka in the freezer.
Or there was.
Maybe you needed it already.
Who can remember at this point?
She doesn't want you to wait for her.
And when she tells you, you don't cry.
You don't scream.
Nothing snaps in your chest.

When this thing started
you were blooming pink with hope.
It was quiet, but it was there.
It was there.
You swear to god it was there.
Now you go home,
open two bottles of wine
and stare at the locks on your door.

Ashe Vernon:

CONVERSATIONS I'M NOT STARTING

11:43am: Hey, this is probably better anyway, right? I mean, nobody who dates me ever sticks around, so now you don't have to find out why.

12:08pm: Do you ever think about how absurd this is? That if I hadn't left that one comment about your mouth on your Instagram picture a year ago, we probably never would have even gotten here? How that one little choice changed the way we talked to each other forever?

12:56pm: We were both so fucking bad at this, weren't we?

3:00pm: I'm sorry but I'm not. Every kind of love that's ever mattered to me has been hundreds of miles away. I'm not sorry for needing someone who could touch me. I'm not sorry for being so tired of being alone.

4:12pm: What does the right version of our love story even look like? Plane tickets every other month? Ten hour road trips? A fistful of flowers and all these kisses goodbye?

4:50pm: I'm willing to admit we got caught up in the myth of one another, but I can't believe that that's all there is to it.

5:24pm: Why else would we shred each other into poetry and call it love?

7:00pm: When I talk about him, I'm afraid to speak too loudly— afraid of rattling your windows, caving in your mailbox, ripping up your garden by the roots. The first time I call him beautiful, I clap my hand over my mouth, like I'm convinced you'll overhear me. I don't want him to become the weapon I use against you, but some nights he feels more knife than boy.

7:01pm: No, fuck—he isn't a knife. Christ, who ever let me get my hands on something as irresponsible as poetry? He's not a knife and you're not a wound and this isn't the scene of a crime, but I guess I am a butcher the way I keep throwing these metaphors around like they could never hurt anyone.

8:05pm: And I feel... I feel like I can't open my mouth without hurting you—like I'm all wrecking ball and fist and I keep aiming for old bruises over and over and over. Like you're painted purple in the shape of my name, like I refuse to let you get over this.

8:08pm: I mean, what if we meet up in Brooklyn and you realize I was never even worth it?

8:10pm: I'm always running away from the people who love me. I'm not saying I made the wrong decision, I'm saying that I'd have found a reason to turn tail and leave even if I never met him.

8:15pm: I'm already trying to run away from him, anyway. I've spent months slipping ghosts into our bed, until every direction he turns looks like leaving. I wanted there to be a problem, so I made one.

8:18pm: I thought you didn't want me and I was wrong. I thought he didn't want me and I was wrong. I refuse to keep being the place where history repeats itself.

9:33pm: So, you and I—we start over. Or we don't start over, but we try again. Who's to say we do it any better than we did the first time? We tucked our first I love yous into poetry. We were better writers than lovers, anyway.

10:15pm: I'm scared that I'll want to kiss you the moment I see you and I'm even more scared that I won't.

2:00am: If the girl you love loves you back but never tells you, does your heartbreak make a sound?

4:45am: I have this dream where I beg you not to go to London. You show up with those hydrangeas and we spend a whole week in bed. But something happens to that boy you still love and, in this world, you never got your unhappy ending and you hate me for keeping you away from him and it's so much worse than falling in love at a distance was. It's so much worse.

Trista Mateer:

ATL AND UNSETTLED SLEEP

So the phone never rings,
but it's okay because I don't wait for it.
Instead, I wonder what a brave face looks like.
I Google how many streets in this new city
are named after peach trees.
I think about kissing other people
and try to want it.

When we work on this book,
I tell myself it's fiction.
She texts at 1am about narrative
and our tired story arc.
I say
it was some other girl
who fucked everything up
and still wakes in the middle of the night
whimpering about bones and sun
and water dripping out of mouths.
I don't know anything about
drinking from cups in the desert.
I've tossed out
all the honey in the house.

Real dream girls, both of us now.
Dismissed as something too delicate
to ever really happen.
Downgraded to a stray thought
that creeps in at night
and has to be gone before morning.

Ashe Vernon:

LINEAR MOTION

Somewhere,
there exists a you and I who have

kissed in more than just poetry,
but there's no proof that they're happy.

Trista Mateer:

ORDER #238935604, or TYING UP LOOSE ENDS

The heart-laid-bare, palms-out fool
closes her hands, crosses her arms, uncrosses her arms.
Wipes her eyes.
Runs her fingers through her hair.
Picks up the phone and calls a florist in Austin, Texas.

*I understand you want to cancel your previous order
for our Joyful Inspirations Blue Hydrangea Bouquet.
Is there anything we can do to change your mind?*

Voice all tremble on the line,
she tries to land a joke
about how hers is not the mind that needs to be changed,
but all that comes out is sugar water.

She does not say, *the flowers mean something different now.
It tries so hard not to be, but blue is the color of forgetting.
The color of a day-after-bruise.
If the flowers show up without me holding them,
it will feel too much like giving something back
that wasn't mine to begin with.*

She swallows mostly everything, and
sobs into the receiver
while the clerk says, *it's okay, it's okay, it's okay.
You'll see a refund on your card in three to five days.*

Ashe Vernon:

VALENTINE'S DAY 2016

The hydrangeas show up on the doorstep
with no girl attached to them.
It's the softest, prettiest kick to the chest.
There's no tag, but you know.

So it's a mistake.
This makes the pill easier to swallow,
but in the end, it still gets stuck
in your throat.

At work, you spend your break
curled up behind your steering wheel,
flowers in the passenger's seat
instead of her.

The first thing you do is call him
and this is how you know, for sure,
that everything is different
from here on in.

Trista Mateer:

POEMS I'M NOT WRITING

Thanks for Nothing, Janelle the Florist

Crying Into Cupcake Batter, but Poetically

I'm Too Sad Not to Make Light of This

It's Not That I Didn't Know Things Were Going This Way,
 It Just Hurts to See It in Print

How Do I Regret Any of This When It Led Me to You?

Ashe Vernon:

UGLY LEFTOVERS or AIRING OUT OLD LAUNDRY

I want to be mad at you.
I want to tell you to *put me down,*
let me go, get my ribs out of your lockjaw.
I want to take you by the shoulders,
want to scream about how
I have been nothing but honest with you—
about what I wanted, and when, and why.
I want to hate all your bite:
how you only hung on when you knew
I was leaving; how you held me at arm's length
right up until I decided to finally walk away;
and then, then you were all *please* and *sorry* and
baby. I want to drive all the way to Atlanta
just to pound on your door and ask
if you have any idea how much it hurt
to be caught between your heartbreak and a soft place;
to be offered up the spoils of love
when I'd already surrendered the war;
for you to show up then
dropping crumpled up love notes on my doorstep,
promising to get on the plane
until I shuddered into panic attack and crumble.
I want—
I want to fall on the floor and kick and scream,
IT ISN'T FAIR. IT ISN'T FAIR.
I don't want to hurt you.
I never wanted to hurt you.
I called this romantic, once.
Now, it just feels messy and ugly and completely avoidable.
I'll never know where to put this overspill of heart.
I want to inherit your reputation for sharp. I want
to hang on and never forgive you for this.
Except—I already have. A hundred times over.
I want to be mad at you.
I'm only mad at myself.

Trista Mateer:

POEMS I'M NOT WRITING (CONT.)

A Dramatic Moment of Clarity

The Poem in Which I Pull Receipts

Remember When I Called Our End Tender?

I Don't Exist to Be Your Ocean of Love, or
  For a Poet, I'm Getting Really Sick of Metaphors

Standing on the Other Side of a Locked Door

I'm Really Very Sorry About the Flowers, or
  Thanks for Nothing, Janelle the Florist Pt. 2

Ashe Vernon:

3 AM, FEBRUARY 15th

The road between his town and mine is as quiet as it ever is.
Which is to say, it isn't. But inside the car, we speak
in hushed voices: afraid of giving heartache the legs to stand on.
The dark makes it easy to be honest. Here, like this, we talk
about the way old love can still blossom into new hurt.
We talk about our fathers.

He sits in the same spot the hydrangeas did. In this light,
he is just as blue. Unlike the flowers, I don't have to pour
the water from the vase to keep him from tipping over.
Unlike the flowers, I don't mind if he needs to.

I don't say,
I like the way your ache understands my ache.
I don't say,
You look beautiful in this light.
I don't say,
You make my heart beat so hard, I can feel it in my teeth.

Instead, I say,
Happy fucking Valentine's Day,
and we laugh in that stubborn, tired way
of people who don't know anything else—
people who've been dragging their past
behind them so long, they don't know
how to put it down.

This is the part of story where
I open the sliding glass door of my chest
and point
and say, *this is where it hurts.*
The part of the story where
he unfurls his body like a fist
and says, *me too.*

Trista Mateer:

POEM IN WHICH I TRY TO DO THE RIGHT THING BUT IT PROBABLY JUST COMES OFF AS BITTER

This is the part of the story where
I bite my tongue, choke on pen ink, put both hands
over my own mouth because it's blooming with poetry
like a basket of roses
(anything but those fucking hydrangeas).

This is the part of the story where
you ask if I'm okay and I know
we've finally come full circle. Again,
I am refusing to tip over somewhere
you might see it.

I'm Fine
is the kindest lie
I know how to tell.

Ashe Vernon:

A CHOICE, IN FIVE PARTS

1.
So, it's morning. Or maybe afternoon. There's light
pouring through the window and it's got him looking
the kind of haloed and soft you only see in movies.
I'm only half awake but I'm already writing poetry
about his eyelashes, can you believe that?

2.
In the mirror, I pretend to watch myself watching myself
brushing my teeth. Instead, I watch him run his hands
through his hair: again and again and again and again.
More than once, I've seen him try to rearrange his body
into negative space. Like one of those optical illusions—
the vase with the two faces. He doesn't know he can be
both of them. He forgets that when you lean too close
to a work of art, the whole picture blurs and disappears.

3.
A new painting: one with no negative space. One where he is
steady hands and solid ground. One with a ukulele and a dog.
Coffee and cayenne. Cheap wine and expensive whiskey. All that
blue in his closet. Him, as the perfect first date and something
soft to come home to. Bad jokes and good intentions
and all that—light.

4.
Listen, so, it's late. Or the time of night some people
call morning. It's dark in the car, but he laughs—
I mean, really laughs: the kind that catches him
by surprise and crinkles up the corners of his eyes,
and it's like a camera flash in a windowless room.
It's the best thing I've seen, all day.

5.
Every morning, the sun has to relearn
how to outshine him. Sometimes
even she is not bright enough.

Trista Mateer:

A WORD OF ADVICE, or THE IMPORTANCE OF LEVEL-HEADED FRIENDS

I say, *I go to bed at night telling myself that it's done and I dream about her anyway. I wake up angry, spend the whole day thinking about where the lines are and how to not cross them.* I say, *the more I try not to think about it, the more it sneaks out at night. My heart is a bad teenager with a ground floor bedroom and no screen in the window. It comes and goes as it pleases. I'm at my wit's end trying to talk sense into it.*

They say, *just lean into it. It isn't doing you any good to pretend to be fine until you get there.* They say, *you're obviously in love with her. That's not going to go away just because it's inconvenient. Sit down with it for a little while. Uncork the bottle, let it get some air.* They say, *it will go away when it wants to. There's no use agonizing over it. So her face makes you feel like you've run a mile out of shape. So her voice chokes you up on the other end of the line. You might just have to let it.*

ILLIAMSBURGH - BROOKLYN. E.D.   St.John's M.E.Ch.   John Wesley M.E.Ch.   Myrtle Ave.   Tompkins Sq   Lefferts Park   Clinton Ave Cong. Ch.
   Williamsburgh Savings Bank   U.S. Naval Hospital   St.James' Cathedral   Simpson Methodist Ch.   Catholic
   Ross St Pedist Ch.   U.S. Marine Barracks   Arsenal   23rd Regt Armory   Kir
   Kings Co.Pen.Ch. U.S.Cob Dock   City Park   Plymouth Ch.   Washington Park
            U.S. Receiving Ship   Wallabout Bay   Navy Yard   Terminus of Bridge, Sands St.
   EAST RIVER BRIDGE   Catherine Ferry-Main St.   EAST RIVER   Fulton Ferry, Fulton St.   Montague Terrace   Bro

THE CITY

COPYRIGHT

EAST NEW YORK.   Flatbush Ave.   Kings County Bldg.   Coney
.. Presbyter Ch.   Tabernacle Ch.   Ridgewood Reservoir   Gowan
        City Hall. Court House   13th Regt Armory   Entrance to Prospect Park.   Flatbush   PROSPECT PARK   Penny Bri
        Ch of the Pilgrims. County Shld. St Annas Ch.   St Public Ch.   Grand Plaza Baptist Ch.   Carroll Park   St Marys' Star of the Sea   Gowan
.. Academy of Music. Packer Institute. Ch of St Charles Borromeo   St Peters Ch.   South Ferry   Atlantic Docks   Governors Isd   Ch of Visitation of B V M
        Fulton St. Ferry, Montague St.   South Ferry. Atlantic Av   La Place W Ch.   Atlantic Basin   Fort Columbus   Cast
                                                              Hamilton Ferry   St Stephens' Ch.   Hamilton Ave.

BROOKLYN.

Ashe Vernon:

MEET ME IN NEW YORK

Across the table at a cafe in Brooklyn,
you have never felt further away.
It is no one's fault, anymore.
We have fault-line ruptured
into two very different people
who are no good at talking to each other.

We laugh into stilted conversation;
we don't poke at anything that hurts.

Look how normal we can be
when we have no other option. See
how we look nothing like two people
who spent months and months
waiting for a kiss
we were never going to get.
What convincing strangers we make.

Turns out, real life
doesn't do neatly packaged endings,
which means this isn't the part
where the music swells,
where we squeeze each other's hands
and the sun sets behind us and it's all
metaphor and credits rolling.
Instead, it's the part where
I pay too much for bad coffee
and we stay on our separate sides
of the table and
resolutely do not touch each other and
convince ourselves we tried our best at this.

Sometimes, an ending is just an ending.
I guess we ran out of things to say.

Trista Mateer:

MEET ME IN NEW YORK B-SIDE

Women Of The World Poetry Slam 2016
Brooklyn, NY

DAY ONE
The first time I ever see you in person, you are sitting on the
floor wearing loud coral leggings. They remind me of poison dart
frogs. I had a book on them when I was younger. I was fascinated
with the way they wore bright colors to warn everyone else off.
When you go in for a hug, I take a visible step backwards. I think,
maybe I just don't have the right colors on. I think, *maybe you need a
crash course in body language.* I think, *maybe it's time to put the
metaphors down.*

DAY TWO
It takes ten minutes for me to break out in stress hives after you
ask me to lunch. I itch in a straight line from collarbone to cheek
and consider it penance for wishing I had your lips there. Across
the table at a cafe, we make a joke out of the awkwardness. You
laugh so hard that you cry and for a moment it's almost like we're
having a real conversation, picking up the heavy things and
putting them on the table instead of tucking them into poetry.
But the moment passes. When we part, I memorize the shape of
you walking away from me just in case I ever need to think about
you again.

DAY THREE
We have dinner with friends and both cradle unsaid words in our
mouths instead of food. When we drop you off, I am painfully
aware that I might never see you again. Tomorrow you go back
to Austin, I go back to Atlanta. Tomorrow I wake up from the
dream of this. Tonight, I say, *bye.* I don't know how to make it
good yet. I watch you walk up the front steps, fumble for your
keys. I think about getting out of the car, calling your name,
giving you that kiss we spent so many months writing about.

DAY FOUR

By the time I wake up, I know you're already gone — on a plane or in an airport somewhere south of here. I tiptoe across the room in the dark, try not to wake the sleeping body in my bed. I sit with your absence on the edge of the tub. Later, when I pack to leave, I don't check the bathroom to see if I've left anything behind.

Ashe Vernon & Trista Mateer:

BEFORE THE FIRST KISS

You showed up in my dream, last night:
cross-legged on the floor with your cheek
against my knee, white light from the window
painting you golden. You were soft and I was sorry.
I braided your hair while we whispered about our
stutter of a love story. You were beautiful.

> I was at the Atlanta airport last week.
> Walking past the Southwest gates. Thinking about
> the last time I sat there, biting my lips, waiting to
> get somewhere. I remembered exactly how it felt
> to be on my way to you for the first time:
> all that anxiety, all that *finally*
> watered down by concourse lemonade
> and a flight delay.

What I mean is, we didn't get our happy ending,
but there's still this whole part of my life
that's dressed in the soft-focus snap of a camera shutter.
Years from now, I'll remember you tasted like summer
even though I never actually got to kiss you.

> What I mean is, it still comes back to sugar water,
> open palms, blushing cheeks.
> It still comes back to blooms and bruises
> in the sun. Bee stings, but not in a bad way.
> Kind of like growing pains.

Maybe someday, we'll be more than just
soft, nervous girls with soft, nervous hands
borrowing each other's favorite clichés.

> Maybe a soft nervous girl
> isn't such a bad thing to be.

AUSTIN,

STATE CAPITAL OF TEXAS.

ABOUT THE AUTHOR

Ashe Vernon is a pansexual poet currently stationed in Austin, Texas with their girlfriend and two cats. Ashe is the author of four full length collections of poetry, including *Wrong Side of a Fistfight* which was nominated for a 2015 Pushcart Prize. Currently working as the Senior Editor of Poetry with *Persephone's Daughters* literary magazine, Ashe is virtually always in the middle of a dozen different projects. They spend their summers touring poetry with their best friend, Jordan Hamilton, and living out of a car for months at a time. Ashe is a very tiny person with very tiny hands and a whole lot to say about it.

(Ashe is agender and recently changed their pronouns from she/her to they/them and asks that any articles or reviews gender them accordingly.)

LATENIGHTCORNERSTORE.COM

ABOUT THE AUTHOR

Trista Mateer is a bisexual poet currently stationed in Austin, Texas with her partner and two cats. Known for her eponymous blog, she is also the author of four full length collections of poetry, and won the Goodreads Choice Award in 2015 for poetry with *The Dogs I Have Kissed*. Her work has been published on *Medium*, *Thought Catalog*, and in *The Rising Phoenix Review*, among other places. She is currently working as a contributing editor at *Words Dance Publishing* and spends most of her time Googling cheap air fare. Once, Buzzfeed referred to her as a "Tumblr darling" and she cried about it.

Contact her at tristamateer@gmail.com or @tristamateer on Twitter!

TRISTAMATEER.COM

WORDS DANCE PUBLISHING has one aim:

To spread mind-blowing / heart-opening poetry.

Words Dance artfully & carefully wrangles words that were born to dance wildly in the heart-mind matrix. Rich, edgy, raw, emotionally-charged energy balled up & waiting to whip your eyes wild; we rally together words that were written to make your heart go boom right before they slay your mind.

Words Dance Publishing is an independent press out of Pennsylvania. We work closely & collaboratively with all of our writers to ensure that their words continue to breathe in a sound & stunning home. Most importantly though, we leave the windows in these homes unlocked so you, the reader, can crawl in & throw one fuck of a house party.

To learn more about our books, authors, events & Words Dance Poetry Magazine, visit:

WORDSDANCE.COM

BELLY OF THE BEAST
Poetry by Ashe Vernon

| $12 | 82 pages | 5.5" x 8.5" | softcover |
ISBN: 978-0692300541

"Into the *Belly of the Beast* we crawl with Ashe as our guide; into the dark visceral spaces where love, lust, descent and desire work their transformative magic and we find ourselves utterly altered in the reading. A truly gifted poet and truth-spiller, Ashe's metaphors create images within images, leading us to question the subjective truths, both shared and hidden, in personal relationship – to the other, and to oneself. Unflinching in her approach, her poetry gives voice to that which most struggle to admit – even if only to themselves. And as such, *Belly of the Beast* is a work of startling courage and rich depth – a darkly delicious pleasure."

— AMY PALKO
Goddess Guide, Digital Priestess & Writer

"It isn't often you find a book of poetry that is as unapologetic, as violent, as moving as this one. Ashe's writing is intense and visceral. You feel the punch in your gut while you're reading, but you don't question it. You know why it's there and you almost welcome it."

— CAITLYN SIEHL
Author of *What We Buried*

"The poems you are about to encounter are the fierce time capsules of girl-hood, girded with sharp elbows, surprise kisses, the meanders of wander-lust. We need voices this strong, this true for the singing reminds us that we are not alone, that someone, somewhere is listening for the faint pulse that is our wish to be seen. Grab hold, this voice will be with us forever."

— RA WASHINGTON
GuidetoKulchurCleveland.com

Titles from
WORDS DANCE PUBLISHING

Crybaby by Caitlyn Siehl
No Matter the Time by Fortesa Latifi
Why I'm Not Where You Are by Brianna Albers
Before the First Kiss by Ashe Vernon & Trista Mateer
Our Bodies & Other Fine Machines by Natalie Wee
Trying to Be a Person by Wesley Scott McMasters
When Minerva's Knees Hit the Ground by Amanda Oaks
A Field of Blooming Bruises by Schuyler Peck
To Break the Heart of the Sun by William Taylor Jr.
Where'd You Put the Keys Girl by Amanda Oaks
The War on Unicorns by Brian James Dawson
The No You Never Listened To by Meggie Royer
Dowry Meat by Heather Knox
Chloe by Kristina Haynes
Belly of the Beast by Ashe Vernon
Shaking the Trees by Azra Tabassum
SparkleFat by Melissa May
What We Buried by Caitlyn Siehl
Love and Other Small Wars by Donna-Marie Riley
What To Do After She Says No by Kris Ryan
No Glass Allowed by Tammy Foster Brewer
Nothing Unrequited Here by Heather Bell
The Map of Our Garden by Rebecca Schumejda
Fossil Fuels by Jessica Dawson
I Eat Crow + Blue Collar at Best by Amanda Oaks + Zach Fishel
Literary Sexts Volumes 1 + 2 : Short & Sexy Love Poems
Poem Your Heart Out Volume 1: Poems, Prompts & Room To Add Your Own

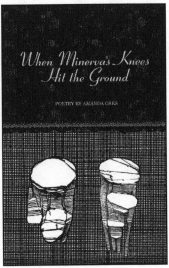

FREE PDF EBOOKS

WHERE'D YOU PUT THE KEYS GIRL + WHEN MINERVA'S KNEES HIT THE GROUND
Poetry by Amanda Oaks

DOWNLOAD HERE:

http://wordsdance.com/free-stuff

Music-inspired digital chapbooks by *Words Dance* Founder, Amanda Oaks. These collections were made with deep love & respect for Tori Amos' + Deftones' music & are made up of erasure poems created from select songs from each artist's catalog + each of the erasure poems are paired an original sister poem & the title of that sister poem is a short lyric from the songs chosen.

"Oaks' original poems, which accompany the erasures, are among the best of her work to date. They are urgent and striking. This is the work of a fully confident poet hitting her stride."

— **KENDALL A. BELL**
Publisher/Editor @ *Maverick Duck Press*

DO YOU WRITE POETRY?
Submit it to our biweekly online magazine!

We publish poems every Tuesday & Thursday on our website.

Come see what all the fuss is about!

We like Poems that sneak up on you. Poems that make out with you. Poems that bloody your mouth just to kiss it clean. Poems that bite your cheek so you spend all day tonguing the wound. Poems that vandalize your heart. Poems that act like a tin can phone connecting you to your childhood. Fire Alarm Poems. Glitterbomb Poems. Jailbreak Poems. Poems that could marry the land or the sea; that are both the hero & the villain. Poems that are the matches when there is a city-wide power outage. Poems that throw you overboard just dive in & save your ass. Poems that push you down on the stoop in front of history's door screaming at you to knock. Poems that are soft enough to fall asleep on. Poems that will still be clinging to the walls inside of your bones on your 90th birthday.

We like poems. Submit yours.

WORDSDANCE.COM

44462798R00067

Made in the USA
San Bernardino, CA
15 January 2017